D0700088

SUPER BOWL CHAMPIONS
PITTSBURGH STEELERS

WIDE RECEIVER
ANTONIO BROWN

Frisch, Aaron, 1975-201
Pittsburgh Steelers /
[2014]
33305231098926
sa   01/16/15

SUPER BOWL CHAMPIONS

PITTSBURGH STEELERS

AARON FRISCH

CREATIVE EDUCATION

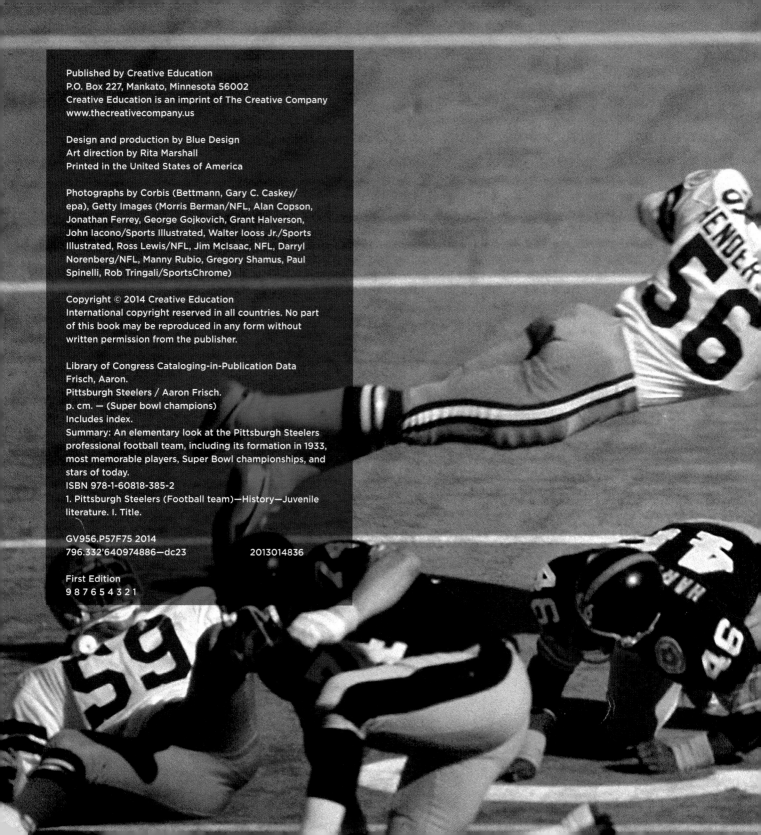

Published by Creative Education
P.O. Box 227, Mankato, Minnesota 56002
Creative Education is an imprint of The Creative Company
www.thecreativecompany.us

Design and production by Blue Design
Art direction by Rita Marshall
Printed in the United States of America

Photographs by Corbis (Bettmann, Gary C. Caskey/
epa), Getty Images (Morris Berman/NFL, Alan Copson,
Jonathan Ferrey, George Gojkovich, Grant Halverson,
John Iacono/Sports Illustrated, Walter Iooss Jr./Sports
Illustrated, Ross Lewis/NFL, Jim McIsaac, NFL, Darryl
Norenberg/NFL, Manny Rubio, Gregory Shamus, Paul
Spinelli, Rob Tringali/SportsChrome)

Copyright © 2014 Creative Education
International copyright reserved in all countries. No part
of this book may be reproduced in any form without
written permission from the publisher.

Library of Congress Cataloging-in-Publication Data
Frisch, Aaron.
Pittsburgh Steelers / Aaron Frisch.
p. cm. — (Super bowl champions)
Includes index.
Summary: An elementary look at the Pittsburgh Steelers
professional football team, including its formation in 1933,
most memorable players, Super Bowl championships, and
stars of today.
ISBN 978-1-60818-385-2
1. Pittsburgh Steelers (Football team)—History—Juvenile
literature. I. Title.

GV956.P57F75 2014
796.332'640974886—dc23   2013014836

First Edition
9 8 7 6 5 4 3 2 1

SUPER BOWL X

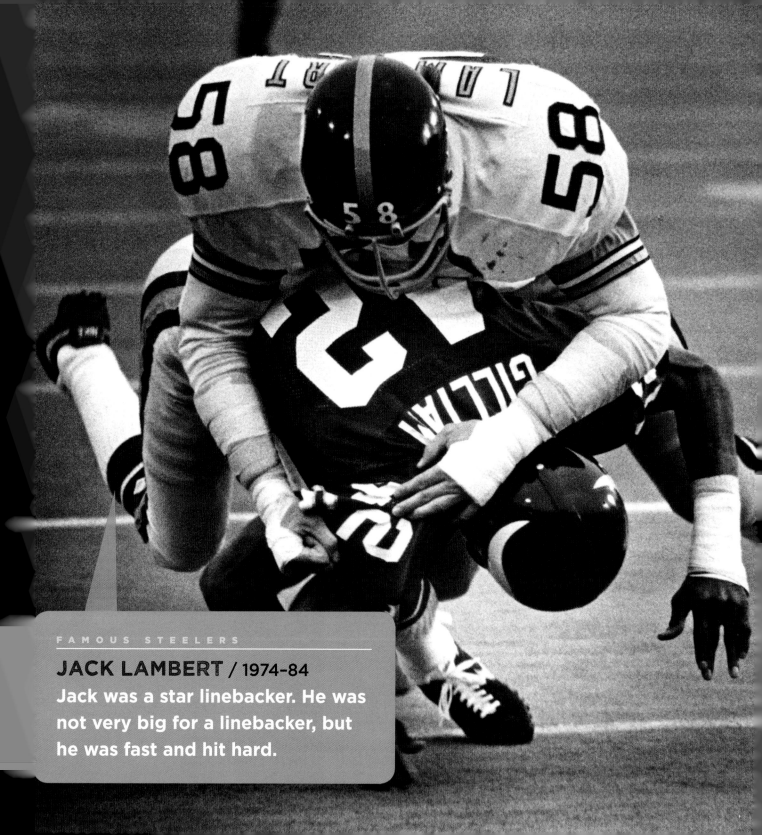

JACK LAMBERT / 1974-84

Jack was a star linebacker. He was not very big for a linebacker, but he was fast and hit hard.

TABLE OF CONTENTS

FAMOUS STEELERS

LYNN SWANN / 1974-82

Lynn was a fast wide receiver. He could run like a deer and leap high to catch passes.

MEN OF STEEL

In the 1930s, Pittsburgh, Pennsylvania, had a football team called the Pirates. The team's owner wanted to change the name. Pittsburgh had many **mills** that made steel. The Pirates became Steelers!

DEFENSIVE END
L. C. GREENWOOD

9

WELCOME TO PITTSBURGH

Pittsburgh is famous for its steel mills. It is famous for its big rivers and bridges, too. Pittsburgh is sometimes called the "Steel City" or the "City of Bridges."

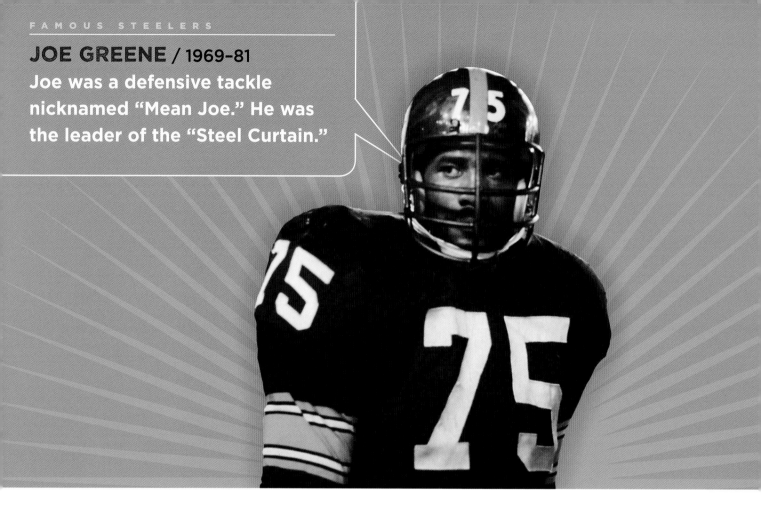

JOE GREENE / 1969–81

Joe was a defensive tackle nicknamed "Mean Joe." He was the leader of the "Steel Curtain."

A LOT OF TROPHIES

By 2013, the Pittsburgh Steelers had won six Super Bowls. That was more than any other National Football League (NFL) team!

FRANCO HARRIS / 1972–83

Franco was Pittsburgh's
main running back during its
championship seasons in the 1970s.

"Some coaches pray for wisdom. I pray for 260-pound tackles. They'll give me plenty of wisdom."
— CHUCK NOLL

THE STEELERS' STORY

The Steelers started out as the Pirates in 1933.
Pittsburgh had some good players like running back
Bill Dudley. But the team could not win any NFL
championships for 40 years.

The Steelers became a **contender** in the 1970s
after they hired coach Chuck Noll. The Steelers'
defense became so tough that fans called it the
"Steel Curtain"!

BILL DUDLEY (#35)

TERRY BRADSHAW

The Steelers won back-to-back Super Bowls after the 1974 and 1975 seasons. Quarterback Terry Bradshaw threw **accurate** passes to lead Pittsburgh's offense.

The Steelers kept winning. They won two more Super Bowls after the 1978 and 1979 seasons. People said the Steelers were the "Team of the '70s."

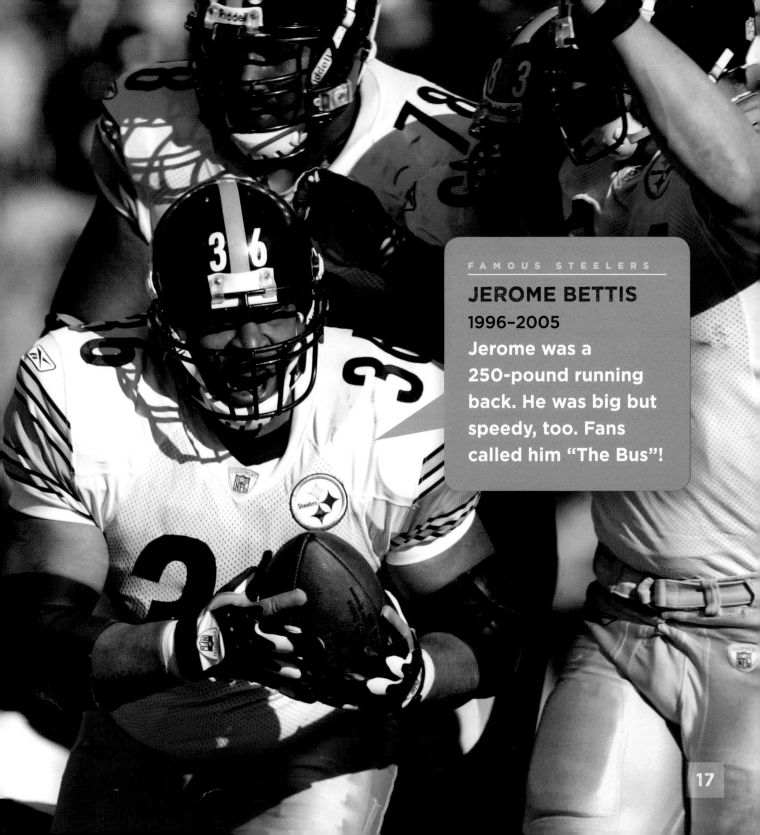

JEROME BETTIS

1996–2005

Jerome was a 250-pound running back. He was big but speedy, too. Fans called him "The Bus"!

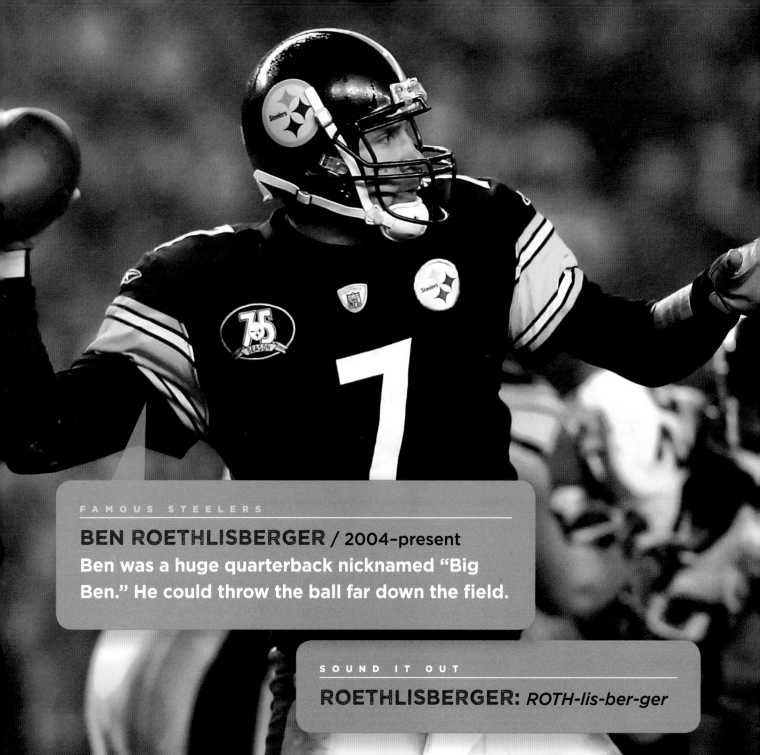

BEN ROETHLISBERGER / 2004–present

Ben was a huge quarterback nicknamed "Big Ben." He could throw the ball far down the field.

SOUND IT OUT

ROETHLISBERGER: *ROTH-lis-ber-ger*

HINES WARD

It took a long time for the Steelers to become champs again. But tough wide receiver Hines Ward helped Pittsburgh win the Super Bowl after the 2005 and 2008 seasons!

By 2013, coach Mike Tomlin was the Steelers' leader. He made sure they always played tough and smart. The Steelers hoped to win a seventh Super Bowl trophy soon!

DEFENSIVE BACK
TROY POLAMALU

FACTS FILE

CONFERENCE/DIVISION:
American Football Conference, North Division

TEAM COLORS:
Black and gold

HOME STADIUM:
Heinz Field

SUPER BOWL VICTORIES:
IX, January 12, 1975 / 16–6 over Minnesota Vikings
X, January 18, 1976 / 21–17 over Dallas Cowboys
XIII, January 21, 1979 / 35–31 over Dallas Cowboys
XIV, January 20, 1980 / 31–19 over Los Angeles Rams
XL, February 5, 2006 / 21–10 over Seattle Seahawks
XLIII, February 1, 2009 / 27–23 over Arizona Cardinals

NFL WEBSITE FOR KIDS:
http://nflrush.com

LINEBACKER LaMARR WOODLEY

GLOSSARY

accurate — on target, or right where something needs to be

contender — a talented team that has a good chance of winning a championship

mills — buildings like factories where machines are used to make food or materials like steel

INDEX

11070005b

Sounds All Around Us

Making Sounds

WITHDRAWN

Charlotte Guillain

Heinemann Library
Chicago, Illinois

www.heinemannraintree.com
Visit our website to find out
more information about
Heinemann-Raintree books.

To order:

☎ Phone 888-454-2279

💻 Visit www.heinemannraintree.com
to browse our catalog and order online.

© 2009 Heinemann Library
an imprint of Capstone Global Library, LLC
Chicago, Illinois

Customer Service: 888-454-2279

Visit our website at www.heinemannraintree.com

All rights reserved. No part of this publication may be reproduced or transmitted in any form or by any means, electronic
or mechanical, including photocopying, recording, taping, or
any information storage and retrieval system, without permission in writing from the publisher.

Designed by Joanna Hinton-Malivoire
Photo research by Tracy Cummins and Tracey Engel
Printed and bound by South China Printing Company Ltd

13 12 11 10 09
10 9 8 7 6 5 4 3 2 1

Library of Congress Cataloging-in-Publication Data
Guillain, Charlotte.
Making sounds / Charlotte Guillain.
p. cm. -- (Sounds around us)
Includes bibliographical references and index.
ISBN 978-1-4329-3200-8 (hc) -- ISBN 978-1-4329-3206-0 (pb)
1. Sound--Juvenile literature. I. Title.
QC225.5.G8498 2008
534--dc22
                    2008051682

Acknowledgments
The author and publishers are grateful to the following for
permission to reproduce copyright material: Alamy pp. **4
top left** (©UpperCut Images), **5** (©Digital Vision), **9** (©Im-
ages of Africa Photobank); ageFotostock pp. **18** (©Creatas),
23a (©Creatas); CORBIS pp. **11** (©TempSpor/Dimitri Iundtt),
23c (©TempSpor/Dimitri Iundtt); Getty Images pp. **6** (©Red
Chopsticks), **7** (©Bernd Opitz), **10** (©Mike Harrington), **12**
(©Ariel Skelley), **16** (©Matthieu Ricard), **19** (©Adam Gault),
23b (©Adam Gault); PhotoEdit Inc. p. **20**; Photolibrary pp.
13 (©Digital Vision), **14** (©Tim Pannell), **15** (©Blend Images RF/Terry Vine/Patrick Lane), **21** (©Digital Vision/Jeffrey
Coolidge Photography), iStockphoto pp. **4 top right** (©Frank
Leung), **4 bottom right** (©Peter Viisimaa); Shutterstock pp. **4
bottom left** (©devi), **8** (©Sonya Etchison), **17** (©Leah-Anne
Thompson).

Cover photograph of Stomp Out Loud cast members reproduced
with permission of Landov (©Reuters/Las Vegas Sun/Steve Mar-
cus). Back cover photograph of a girl kicking leaves reproduced
with permission of Getty Images (©Mike Harrington).

The publishers would like to thank Nancy Harris and Adriana
Scalise for their assistance in the preparation of this book.

Every effort has been made to contact copyright holders of any
material reproduced in this book. Any omissions will be
rectified in subsequent printings if notice is given to the publisher.

Contents

Sounds

There are many different sounds.

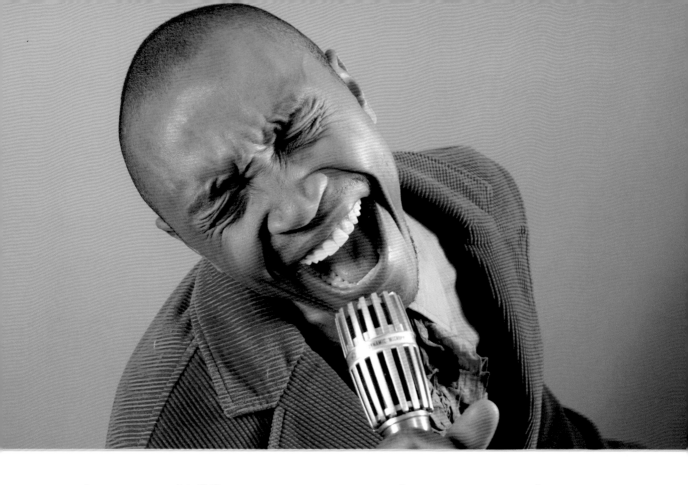

We hear different sounds around us every day.

Sounds Our Bodies Make

We can make many different sounds.

We can use our bodies to
make sounds.

We can use our hands to
make sounds.

We can clap our hands.

We can use our feet to make sounds.

We can stamp our feet.

We can use our voices to
make sounds.

We can use our voices to sing.

We can use our voices to shout.

We can use our voices to whisper.

We can use our mouths to
make sounds.

We can use our mouths to whistle.

Other Sounds We Can Make

We can bang things to make sounds.

We can scrape things to make sounds.

We can shake things to make sounds.

We can press things to make sounds.

What Have You Learned?

- We can use our hands to make sounds.

- We can use our feet to make sounds.

- We can use our mouths and voices to make sounds.

- We can make sounds using many other things.

Picture Glossary

 **bang** sudden loud noise

 **scrape** rub against something hard or rough

 **stamp** bring your foot down firmly on the ground

Index

Note to Parents and Teachers

Before reading

Tell children that there are sounds all around us every day. Explain that there are different ways we can make sounds using our bodies and other things. Ask children to discuss ways of making different sounds and to make a list of their ideas.

After reading

• Look back at the list with the children. Ask volunteers to circle sounds that were in the book. Then have a few children make that sound with their bodies or things in the class.

• Pass around musical instruments and have children make their own sounds. Instruct them to play their instruments loudly and quietly. Ask them what they had to do to make loud and quiet sounds.

31901047005485